D1499899

MAR 18 2015

TEMPLE TIMES

BLAME THE BOYS

HELEN OF TROY TELLS ALL

by Nancy Loewen

illustrated by Stephen Gilpin

SHIP SHORTAGE IN SPARTA!

HELEN THE DESTROYER: "C'mon, now. For real? Me?!"

PICTURE WINDOW BOOKS
a capstone imprint

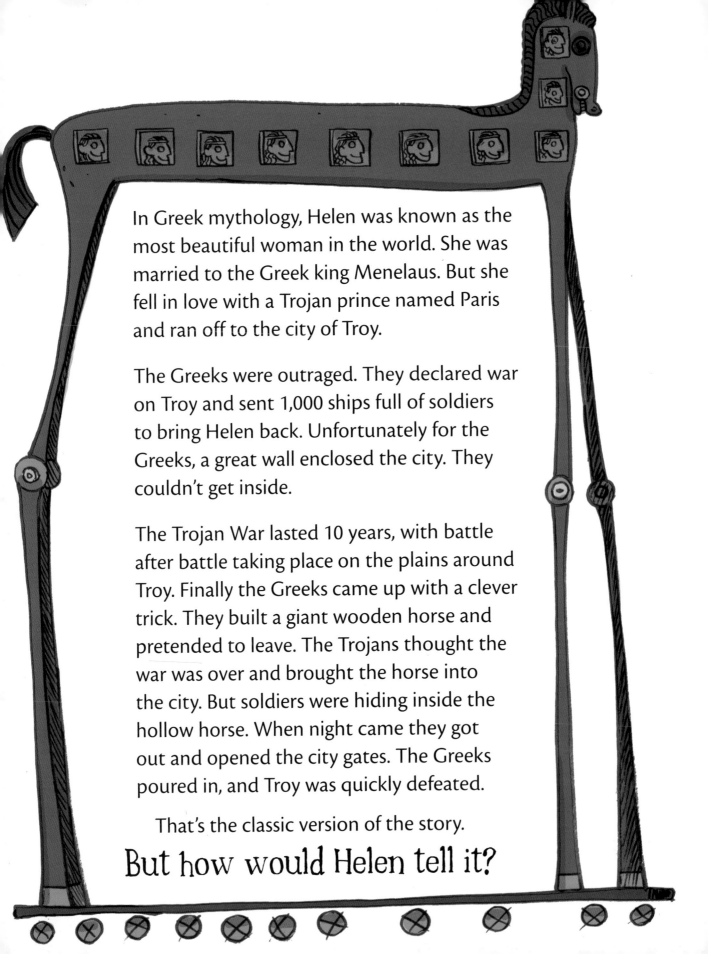

In Greek mythology, Helen was known as the most beautiful woman in the world. She was married to the Greek king Menelaus. But she fell in love with a Trojan prince named Paris and ran off to the city of Troy.

The Greeks were outraged. They declared war on Troy and sent 1,000 ships full of soldiers to bring Helen back. Unfortunately for the Greeks, a great wall enclosed the city. They couldn't get inside.

The Trojan War lasted 10 years, with battle after battle taking place on the plains around Troy. Finally the Greeks came up with a clever trick. They built a giant wooden horse and pretended to leave. The Trojans thought the war was over and brought the horse into the city. But soldiers were hiding inside the hollow horse. When night came they got out and opened the city gates. The Greeks poured in, and Troy was quickly defeated.

That's the classic version of the story.

But how would Helen tell it?

I am the most beautiful
woman in the world.

It's a fact.

I try to hide my beauty sometimes. I go around in
mismatched clothes and don't wash my hair for days. It
doesn't matter—men take one look at me and fall in love.

But enough about how beautiful I am. This is a story
about war—a war that everyone blames *on me*. And I'm
telling you, the Trojan War was NOT my fault!

It all started when I became old enough to marry. Every man in the kingdom wanted me as his wife. Very few of them had a chance, but that didn't stop them from boasting and brawling.

"This is crazy," my dad, King Tyndareus, said as we watched yet another fight break out. "Can't you wear a mask or something? Maybe grow a beard?"

I just glared at him.

"They'll all end up killing each other, and we won't have any soldiers left! I've got to do something," he said.

The next day my dad made a decree.

Any man wishing to be considered a husband for Helen must solemnly swear to:

A) support the man who is chosen; and

B) defend Helen against anyone who might try to steal her away.

Of course, all the men wanted to believe that they were still in the running, so they all made that promise. The fighting stopped.

I married Menelaus and became Queen of Sparta.
We had a little girl named Hermione.

Life was good.

Then one day we had a visitor from across the ocean.
His name was Paris.

"My dear Helen," he said as we were introduced,
"I've been waiting my whole life for this moment."

I tried not to roll my eyes.

Then—ZING!

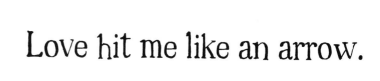

Love hit me like an arrow.

Before long I'd packed my things and sailed off to Troy with my new love.

I know, I know. It looks bad. But here's the thing: Paris had made a bargain with Aphrodite, the goddess of love and beauty, and I was powerless to stop it.

You see, Aphrodite had offered Paris the most beautiful woman in the world. (That's me, of course!) All he had to do was pick Aphrodite as the winner in a beauty contest among the goddesses. So that's what he did.

KWAPING!

To make sure I went along with the plan, Aphrodite had her son Eros shoot me with one of his love arrows. Let me tell you, those arrows could make a person fall in love with an old shoe! (Honestly, I wish I *had* fallen in love with an old shoe. It would have saved a lot of trouble.)

Paris and I had barely gotten settled when we heard that Menelaus was coming to get me.

"And he's not alone," Paris said, his face pale. "Word is, a thousand ships are heading this way!"

"My old suitors," I whispered. "They made a promise to my dad."

Even then we could have avoided war, if only the Trojans hadn't been so stubborn. They refused to give me up. The war began.

Inside the city we were safe. A high, sturdy wall protected Troy. But every morning the men went out to fight, and not everyone made it back in the evening.

This went on for 10 YEARS.

I was miserable. Everyone hated me—Greeks and Trojans alike. Paris was killed by a poisoned arrow. And still the fighting went on …

One morning a hush was in the air. People gathered in the streets. "The Greeks went away!" they said. "We won!"

A giant wooden horse stood just outside the city. A scruffy-looking Greek soldier stood beside it. "They left me behind," he said in disbelief. "What a rotten thing to do! My snoring isn't *that* bad."

He said the Greeks had built the horse as a gift for the goddess Athena. As long as the horse stayed outside the city walls, Athena would smile upon them and lead them to victory.

"Obviously we were wrong," the soldier said. "You won. You might as well take it. Enjoy!"

The Trojans hauled the big horse inside Troy's walls. Finally the war was over.

That night I woke with a start. Outside, people were yelling—weapons clanging—it was awful.

The horse was a trick! Greek soldiers had been hiding in it all day. When night came they jumped out and opened the gates for the rest of their troops. Troy didn't have a chance.

23

My husband, Menelaus, found me. He was dirty and exhausted. And mad—so mad that he drew his sword on me.

I took a deep breath and focused all my thoughts on my dazzling beauty. If ever I needed to put a man into a trance, it was then! I smoothed back my hair and held my hand out to him.

"Don't, Menelaus," I said softly. "I didn't want all this to happen. Please believe me. And please take me home. I'm yours again."

Whew! That did the trick. Menelaus and I were back together. We sailed for home.

25

All the stories say that it was my running off with Paris that caused the Trojan War. That it was my fault. That I was selfish. But what could I have done differently? The way I see it, the blame should go to:

My dad, for making all those silly suitors promise to defend me.

Aphrodite, for promising me to Paris when I was already married.

Paris, for being greedy. He should have known that claiming me would lead to disaster.

Aphrodite's son Eros. Love arrows should be banned!

The stubborn Trojans, for not letting me go when they had the chance.

Well, what's done is done. There's nothing I can do about it now.

Just do me a favor, OK? When you hear stories about boys fighting over a girl, don't blame the girl. She probably didn't have anything to do with it!

Critical Thinking Using the Common Core ★ ★ ★ ★ ★ ★

This version of the classic Greek myth "The Wooden Horse" is told by Helen, from her point of view. If Paris told the story, what details might he tell differently? What if Menelaus told the story from his point of view? (Integration of Knowledge and Ideas)

Helen claims that she had nothing to do with the Trojan War, that she was put under a spell by Eros' love arrow. Who does she blame for the Trojan War? And what should they have done differently? (Key Ideas and Details)

Describe the steps the Greek soldiers took to get inside the walls of Troy. (Craft and Structure)

Glossary ★

Aphrodite—the Greek goddess of love and beauty

brawl—to fight in a noisy, rough way

decree—a formal order given by a person in power

defeat—to beat someone in a competition

enclose—to surround

mortal—human, referring to a being who will eventually die

mythology—old or ancient stories told again and again that help connect people with their past

point of view—a way of looking at something

Sparta—a city-state in Ancient Greece known for its strong army

suitor—a man who is courting, or dating, a woman

trance—a state of being dazed and easily swayed

version—an account of something from a certain point of view

Read More ★★★★★★★★★★★★★★★★★★

Bensinger, Henry. *Ancient Greek Daily Life.* Spotlight on Ancient Civilizations: Greece. New York: Rosen Publishing Group, 2014.

Cline, Eric, and Jill Rubalcaba. *Digging for Troy: From Homer to Hisarlik.* Watertown, Mass.: Charlesbridge, 2011.

Llanas, Sheila Griffin. *Helen of Troy.* Queens and Princesses. Mankato, Minn.: Capstone Press, 2009.

Meister, Cari. *The Wooden Horse of Troy: A Retelling by Cari Meister.* Mankato, Minn.: Picture Window Books, 2012.

Internet Sites ★★★★★★★★★★★★★★★★★★

FactHound offers a safe, fun way to find Internet sites related to this book. All of the sites on FactHound have been researched by our staff.

Here's all you do:

Visit *www.facthound.com*

Type in this code: 9781479521821

 Check out projects, games and lots more at **www.capstonekids.com**

Thanks to our advisers for their expertise, research, and advice:

Susan C. Shelmerdine, PhD, Professor of Classical Studies
University of North Carolina, Greensboro

Terry Flaherty, PhD, Professor of English
Minnesota State University, Mankato

Editor: Jill Kalz
Designer: Lori Bye
Art Director: Nathan Gassman
Production Specialist: Kathy McColley
The illustrations in this book were created digitally.

Picture Window Books are published by Capstone,
1710 Roe Crest Drive, North Mankato, Minnesota 56003
www.capstonepub.com

Copyright © 2015 by Picture Window Books, a Capstone imprint.
All rights reserved. No part of this publication may be reproduced in whole or in
part, or stored in a retrieval system, or transmitted in any form or by any means,
electronic, mechanical, photocopying, recording, or otherwise, without written
permission of the publisher.

Library of Congress Cataloging-in-Publication Data
Loewen, Nancy, 1964–
  Helen of troy tells all : blame the boys / by Nancy Loewen; illustrated by
Stephen Gilpin.
    pages cm.—(Nonfiction picture books. The other side of the myth.
  Summary: "Introduces the concept of point of view through Helen of Troy's
retelling of the classic Greek myth 'The Wooden Horse'"—Provided by publisher.
  ISBN 978-1-4795-2182-1 (library binding)
  ISBN 978-1-4795-2939-1 (paperback)
  ISBN 978-1-4795-3318-3 (eBook PDF)
1. Helen of Troy (Greek mythology)—Juvenile literature. I. Gilpin, Stephen
illustrator. II. Title.
  BL820.H45L46 2014
  398.20938'02—dc23
                              2013046714

photo credit: Hugo-Gunn Photography

About the Author

Nancy Loewen writes fiction and nonfiction for
children and young adults. Recent awards include:
2013 Oppenheim Toy Portfolio Best Book Award
(*Baby Wants Mama*); 2012 Minnesota Book Awards
finalist (*The LAST Day of Kindergarten*); and 2010
AEP Distinguished Achievement Award (Writer's
Toolbox series). She's also received awards from
the American Library Association, the New York
Public Library, and the Society of School Librarians
International. Nancy holds an MFA in creative writing
from Hamline University. She lives in Minneapolis.
Visit www.nancyloewen.com to learn more.

Look for all the books in the series:

CRONUS THE TITAN TELLS ALL: TRICKED BY THE KIDS
CYCLOPS TELLS ALL: THE WAY EYE SEE IT
HELEN OF TROY TELLS ALL: BLAME THE BOYS
MEDEA TELLS ALL: A MAD. MAGICAL LOVE
MEDUSA TELLS ALL: BEAUTY MISSING. HAIR HISSING
PANDORA TELLS ALL: NOT THE CURIOUS KIND

Printed in the United States of America in North Mankato, Minnesota.
032014   008087CGF14